weezer fan

PHASE 7 #017-#019

weezer fan

PHASE 7 #017-#019

Alec Longstreth

PHASE SEVEN COMICS

PLEASE NOTE:

I HAVE MOVED SINCE I SELF-PUBLISHED THESE MINICOMICS. PLEASE CHECK MY WEBSITE TO GET MY **CURRENT** CONTACT INFORMATION BEFORE YOU SEND ME ANY MAIL. THANKS!

WEEZER FAN : PHASE 7 #017-#019

ENTIRE CONTENTS (INCLUDING ALL STORIES, CHARACTERS AND ART) COPYRIGHT ©2013-2014 ALEC LONGSTRETH, **UNLESS OTHERWISE NOTED!** NO PART OF THIS BOOK MAY BE REPRODUCED WITHOUT THE WRITTEN CONSENT OF ALEC LONGSTRETH.

ISBN 978-0-9853004-8-7

#017 - $4.00

ALEC LONGSTRETH

ISSUE SEVENTEEN
P.O. BOX 11207 OAKLAND, CA 94611
alec@alec-longstreth.com

YIKES! 2012 WAS A VERY BUSY YEAR FOR ME. I SPENT THE FIRST FIVE MONTHS OF IT FILLING IN AS THE ACTING DIRECTOR OF THE CENTER FOR CARTOON STUDIES, WHILE JAMES STURM WAS ON A WELL-EARNED SABBATICAL. SOON THEREAFTER CLAIRE AND I PACKED UP ALL OF OUR WORLDLY POSSESSIONS AND MOVED FROM WHITE RIVER JUNCTION, VERMONT TO OAKLAND, CALIFORNIA. IRONICALLY, I THEN RETURNED TO VERMONT FOR THE SUMMER, TO HELP TEACH THE CCS SUMMER WORKSHOPS. IN AUGUST I CAME HOME TO OAKLAND ONCE AND FOR ALL.

DURING ALL OF THIS ACTIVITY I MANAGED TO SCRIPT OUT THE NEXT THREE ISSUES OF PHASE 7, WHICH I AM CALLING MY "WEEZER FAN TRILOGY." YOU ARE HOLDING PART ONE IN YOUR HANDS RIGHT NOW! WHILE IT IS NOT NECESSARY FOR YOU TO HAVE HEARD WEEZER'S "BLUE ALBUM" TO ENJOY THIS COMIC BOOK, I WILL SAY THAT IF YOU HAVE **NOT** HEARD THE BLUE ALBUM, YOU ARE MISSING OUT ON ONE OF THE GREATEST ALBUMS EVER RECORDED! AS YOU READ ON, YOU WILL SEE THAT I CAN NOT RECOMMEND IT HIGHLY ENOUGH!

I AM TRYING OUT SOME NEW TECHNIQUES IN THIS ISSUE, WHICH I HOPE WILL ALLOW ME TO PRODUCE ISSUES IN A MORE TIMELY MANNER. IT WAS A QUIET 2012 FOR ME ON THE COMICS FRONT, BUT I'M HOPING 2013 WILL MAKE UP FOR IT. IN GENERAL, I'M TRYING TO HAVE MORE **FUN** WITH MY COMICS NOW THAT BASEWOOD IS DONE, AND THIS ISSUE IS A BIG STEP IN THAT DIRECTION!

—ALEC LONGSTRETH   OAKLAND, CA

PHASE 7 #017 – FEBRUARY 2013. ENTIRE CONTENTS (INCLUDING ALL ART AND STORIES) COPYRIGHT ©2013 BY ALEC LONGSTRETH, UNLESS OTHERWISE NOTED (FOR INSTANCE, **BELOW**). NO PART OF THIS PUBLICATION (EXCEPT SINGLE PANELS FOR REVIEW PURPOSES) MAY BE REPRODUCED WITHOUT THE WRITTEN PERMISSION OF ALEC LONGSTRETH. DEAR GEFFEN, PLEASE DO NOT SUE ME!
FIRST PRINTING – 550 COPIES

BONUS! BLUE ALBUM CREDITS: ALL SONGS WRITTEN BY RIVERS CUOMO, PUBLISHED BY E.O. SMITH MUSIC (BMI) EXCEPT AS NOTED: TRACK 1 WRITTEN BY RIVERS CUOMO, PATRICK WILSON, AND JASON CROPPER, PUBLISHED BY E.O. SMITH MUSIC (BMI), FIE! PUBLISHING (BMI), AND UBER-MOMMASUPRAPOPPA MUSIC (BMI). TRACKS 3 AND 6 WRITTEN BY RIVERS CUOMO AND PATRICK WILSON, PUBLISHED BY E.O. SMITH MUSIC (BMI) AND FIE! PUBLISHING (BMI)

weezer fan

PART ONE *by* ALEC LONGSTRETH

WEEZER'S SELF-TITLED DEBUT (KNOWN AS "THE BLUE ALBUM") WAS RELEASED ON MAY 10TH, 1994.

AT THE TIME, I WAS FOURTEEN YEARS OLD, THOUGH I DIDN'T ACTUALLY OWN THE ALBUM UNTIL ABOUT A YEAR LATER....

AS THE OPENING BARS OF "MY NAME IS JONAS" BLASTED OUT OF THE SPEAKERS, I REALIZED A NUMBER OF THINGS SIMULTANEOUSLY:

1) THIS WAS MY FIRST TIME RIDING IN A CAR WITHOUT AN ADULT.

2) I HAD NEVER LISTENED TO MUSIC TURNED UP THIS **LOUD** BEFORE.

AND 3) THEY HADN'T ASKED ME WHERE I LIVED!

2. No one else

I LISTENED TO THE BLUE ALBUM **CONSTANTLY**. IN NO TIME, I KNEW ALL OF THE LYRICS BY HEART.

MYYY GIRL'S GOTTA BIG MOUTH WITH WHICH SHE BLABBERS A LOT!

THEN I STARTED SINGING ALL THE HARMONIES, THE GUITAR SOLOS, THE BASS LINES, AND ALL THE DRUM FILLS.

REEARNGH! BA-DAT DAT DATTA **SPASH**!

WHEN I COULDN'T LISTEN TO THE BLUE ALBUM IT WAS STILL PLAYING NON-STOP IN MY HEAD.

SHEEE LAUGHS AT MOST EVERYTHING WHETHER IT'S FUNNY OR NOT!

IT FELT LIKE THE MUSIC WAS ON **FIRE** INSIDE OF ME AND IT WAS TRYING TO GET OUT!

DO DOO WOODO WOO!

SINGING ALONG WAS NO LONGER CUTTING IT. I HAD TO **MAKE** THIS MUSIC.

MOM, CAN I **PLEASE** GET A GUITAR FOR CHRISTMAS?

≡SIGH≡

I GUESS GALEN HAD **ALSO** ASKED FOR A GUITAR FOR CHRISTMAS, SO MY PARENTS FOUND A TWO-FOR-ONE DEAL AT A LOCAL MUSIC SHOP.

WOW!

THANKS MOM AND DAD!

THANK SANTA CLAUS!

I TAUGHT MYSELF HOW TO PLAY THE GUITAR BY LEARNING ALL OF THE SONGS ON THE BLUE ALBUM.

IT WAS SUCH A WONDERFUL FEELING, BEING ABLE TO CREATE ACOUSTIC VERSIONS OF MY FAVORITE SONGS ALL BY MYSELF.

AAAND IF YOU SEE HER, TELL HER IT'S OVER NOW!

WHEN I LEFT FOR COLLEGE, I FOOLISHLY DECIDED TO KEEP DATING MY HIGH SCHOOL GIRLFRIEND LONG DISTANCE.

A MONTH BEFORE THE END OF MY FRESHMAN YEAR, SHE TOLD ME SHE HAD BEEN CHEATING ON ME WITH A FRIEND OF HERS.

3. The World has turned and left me here

Pretty soon after my sister gave me the blue album, I signed up to be a member of the Weezer fan club.

"Alec, it looks like you got some mail from Portland."

"Huh?!"

The fan club was run by two sisters: Mykel and Carli Allen. When you signed up they sent you a membership card and a photo of the band, signed by all of the guys.

"Oh my god, this is SO cool!!!"

I also got the latest issue of **WEEZINE**, which was the first thing I ever read that was self-published.

Has no idea that in seven years he will be obsessed with making zines of his own.

"Huh!"

Mykel and Carli also sent out a Weezer fan club directory, with the addresses of all the fans, listed by state.

"Hmm... let's see, Washington..."

When I was listed in an updated directory a few months later, I began writing letters with other local Weezer fans.

PRE-EMAIL

The first time I met another fan clubber in person was during high school, at my friend Tyler's house.

4. Buddy Holly

Weezer's most popular song is "Buddy Holly," thanks in part to its award-winning video which was directed by Spike Jonze.

"HAPPY DAYS" THEME →

Windows '95 came with a digital copy of the video, but my family only owned Apple computers.

QUADRA 650

It was also played a lot on MTV, but my family never had cable.

ONLY 7 CHANNELS

=SIGH=

I first saw the video when one of my Weezer fan club pen pals sent me a VHS tape loaded with all kinds of Weezer videos and TV appearances.

I watched that tape **a lot** in high school!

REWIND!

Buddy Holly is still played on the radio today, and it is often the only available Weezer song at karaoke bars.

"What are you going to sing?"

"Guess!"

"Ha ha, I know!"

6. Surf Wax America

MY HIGH SCHOOL HAD A RADIO STATION: **KMIH** 104.5 FM.

GALEN HAD A LOT OF FUN IN RADIO CLUB WHEN SHE WAS IN HIGH SCHOOL, SO BY THE TIME I GOT THERE, I ALREADY KNEW I WANTED TO BE INVOLVED.

AT MY FIRST MEETING, I WAS PAIRED WITH **GREG GARCIA**, WHO WAS A FEW YEARS OLDER THAN ME, FOR MY TRAINING.

"OKAY, PICK OUT SOME MUSIC AND I'LL SHOW YOU HOW ALL THIS STUFF WORKS."

GREG WAS ALSO THE DRUMMER IN JAZZ BAND. I THOUGHT HE WAS **VERY** COOL.

"**WEEZER**, EH? NICE PICK!"

EVENTUALLY, I HAD TO TAKE A TEST, AND THEN A FEW WEEKS LATER MY F.C.C. LICENSE SHOWED UP.

ALEX LONGSTRETH

AS THE NEW GUY, I GOT ONE OF THE LATER TIME SLOTS FOR MY RADIO SHOW.

"THANKS MOM. SEE YOU IN A COUPLE OF HOURS."

"SO UNTIL NEXT WEEK THIS IS **INGER ADAIR** SIGNING OFF!"

23

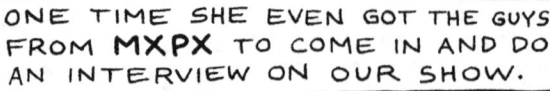

7. Say it ain't so

Each member of Weezer grew up in a different place, but the band was originally formed in **Los Angeles** on Valentine's Day, 1992.

- Pat Wilson — Buffalo, NY
- Rivers Cuomo — Pomfret, CT
- Matt Sharp — Arlington, VA
- Brian Bell — Knoxville, TN

Ten years later, I found **myself** moving to Los Angeles, after I graduated from college.

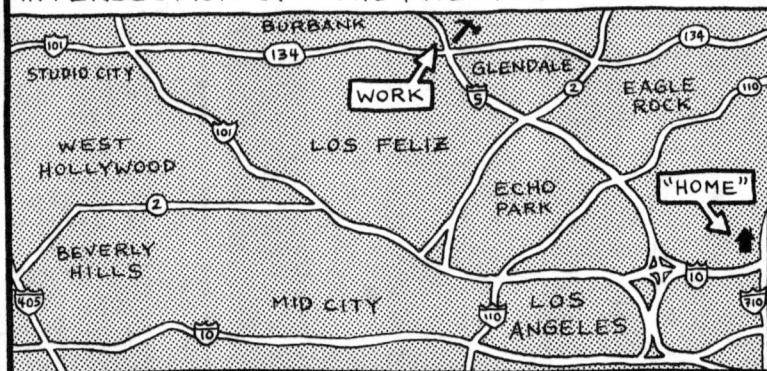

I got a job building sets up in Glendale and an apartment right next to the intersection of "the Five" and "the Ten."

I usually drove to work at about 5:30 in the morning. It took me fifteen minutes door to door.

When I drove home in the afternoon, it took **forty-five** minutes, and if I had to work late it could take more than an hour!

9. Holiday

WHEN I GOT MY DRIVER'S LICENSE IN HIGH SCHOOL, MY PARENTS LET ME DRIVE THEIR 1986 CHEVY CELEBRITY STATION WAGON.

BACKWARDS FACING SEAT

AM RADIO **ONLY**, NO TAPE DECK

SAFELY SEATS EIGHT PEOPLE

MAROON

WHEN I LEFT FOR COLLEGE, THEY SOLD THE CAR.

JULIE

UNLUCKILY, MY FIRST COLLEGE COMPUTER WAS A LEMON. LUCKILY, I HAD A "RESIDENTIAL COMPUTING CONSULTANT" LIVING DOWN THE HALL IN MY DORM.

AFTER HE CHECKED OUT MY COMPUTER, WE WENT BACK TO HIS ROOM TO FILL OUT SOME FORMS SO THAT I COULD GET A NEW COMPUTER.

UP ON A HIGH, EMPTY SHELF HE HAD PLACED HIS CASSETTE TAPE OF THE BLUE ALBUM, FACE OUT. I KNEW AS SOON AS I SAW IT THAT WE WOULD BE FRIENDS.

LETTERS
P.O. BOX 11207 OAKLAND, CA 94611

NOTE: LETTERS TO PHASE 7 BECOME PROPERTY OF THE COMIC AND ARE ASSUMED INTENDED FOR PUBLICATION IN WHOLE OR IN PART (UNLESS OTHERWISE INDICATED).

HEY... YOU SENT IT A COUPLE WEEKS AGO, BUT I FINALLY GOT AROUND TO READING THE FINAL CHAPTER OF BASEWOOD TODAY.

IT WAS PRETTY EMOTIONAL TO READ IT. ESPECIALLY THE END, WHEN THINGS GET ACTION PACKED. THAT WAS AWESOME. BUT THE PARTS WHERE KINDA TIME WAS JUST PASSING WORDLESSLY WERE EMOTIONAL TOO, BECAUSE I FOUND MY MIND REFLECTING ON YOUR LONG JOURNEY DRAWING THIS WORK.

I'M TREMENDOUSLY PROUD OF YOU. PLENTY OF FOLKS JUST QUIT THEIR BIG PROJECTS LONG BEFORE COMPLETING THEM. AND I'M TREMENDOUSLY HONORED THAT YOU BROUGHT ME ALONG ON THIS JOURNEY WITH YOU. THANK YOU SO MUCH FOR SENDING ME EACH NEW ISSUE AS IT CAME OUT.

BEST WISHES & HAPPY NEW YEAR,
JAMES KOCHALKA

THANKS SO MUCH FOR YOUR KIND WORDS, JAMES. IT MEANS A LOT TO ME THAT YOU ENJOYED BASEWOOD, BECAUSE YOUR COMICS WERE SOME OF THE MAIN ONES I READ THAT MADE ME WANT TO DRAW MY OWN. IF PEOPLE DON'T KNOW, JAMES IS THE FIRST CARTOONIST LAUREATE OF VERMONT STATE! YOU CAN READ 14 YEARS OF HIS DAILY DIARY COMICS AT:
www.americanelf.com
OR YOU CAN CHECK OUT **DOZENS** OF HIS GRAPHIC NOVELS AND COMIC BOOKS AT:
www.topshelfcomix.com

ALEC,
JUST FINISHED READING BASEWOOD IN ITS ENTIRETY. IT MUST BE STRANGE TO HEAR THAT, KNOWING THAT A 12 YEAR JOURNEY FOR YOU CAN BE CONSUMED IN AN EVENING. I PREFER TO THINK THAT YOU'VE CREATED A STORY CAPTIVATING ENOUGH THAT SOMEONE WOULD WANT TO READ IT IN ONE FELL SWOOP. BASEWOOD KEPT ME UP LONG PAST MY BED TIME — ONLY THE BEST KINDS OF STORIES DO THAT.

I COULD GUSH AT LENGTH OVER THE INSANELY WELL-RENDERED SNOW SCENES IN CHAPTER THREE OR THE SATISFYING HATCHING AND STIPPLING THROUGHOUT, BUT I'LL LEAVE THAT TO YOUR OTHER READERS. I WANTED TO HIGHLIGHT IN THIS LETTER AN ASPECT OF BASEWOOD THAT I THINK KEPT ME PERSONALLY TURNING THE PAGES. AS A KID I WAS OBSESSED WITH BUILDING THINGS. WHETHER IT WAS LEGOS, STICKS OR RECYCLED MATERIALS, I LOVED THE IDEA OF TAKING SOMETHING OUT OF YOUR IMAGINATION AND GIVING IT LIFE THROUGH RANDOM SCRAPS AND SCREWS. YOU EXPLORE THAT LOVE OF BUILDING THROUGHOUT BASEWOOD FROM THE VERY FIRST PAGES TO ITS COMPLETION. WHETHER IT'S FASHIONING A SHOE OUT OF TREE BARK, BUILDING A HOUSE HIGH UP IN THE TREES OR CREATING A WINDMILL AT THE EDGE OF A CLIFF, YOUR ABILITY TO SHOW THE BUILDING PROCESS STEP-BY-STEP AND TO DO IT IN SUCH A SATISFYING WAY HAD ME COMPLETELY ENGROSSED. I HOPE TO SEE MORE OF THIS FROM YOU IN THE FUTURE. EVEN IF YOU JUST RELEASED A COMIC CALLED "ALEC BUILDS THINGS" AND EACH CHAPTER WAS YOU BUILDING A DIFFERENT CREATION OUT OF WHAT WAS randomly available, I wouldn't be able to put it down.

I hope your journey through Basewood is something you continue to look back on with pride. And even though it only took me a night to make that journey myself, it was a great night. Thanks for that.

Keep inking forward,
Luke Howard

> I'm glad to know you enjoyed the building scenes, Luke, and that Basewood was engrossing enough to keep you up at night. I love the imbalanced creation-to-consumption ratio of comics, I just hope I can draw faster so that I can share **MORE** of my stories with people. While everyone is waiting for my next comic, they should head to **LUKE'S** site to check out some of his! www.andsothen.com

Alec —

Thanks for a great time last night. It was certainly a singular release party.

You had shared during the release party the general sense that you overcommitted to a certain style in Basewood that was time-consuming and challenging. It tested your resolve to finish the project. You talked about people responding that your comic was insanely complex and your peers could ink pages at a blinding speed compared to your work. It was a learning point for you and an indicator of how you would change your approach to future work.

Shortly after I left your party I spent the rest of the evening with a widower who lost his wife to cancer about three weeks ago. He is still grieving and missing his wife. We talked about how they shared the last months together and the amount of work and effort that was necessary to care for her from food to medications to general hygiene. He did not question his efforts for one minute. He was and continues to be completely devoted to his wife — an enduring example of committed love.

After helping him consume approximately a liter of Southern Comfort I stumbled home and spent the rest of the evening reading through Basewood. It was the first time I really paid attention to your hard work and the incredible detail. It is astonishing and entrancing (at this moment my three eldest children, 5 to 9 years old, are crowded around the kitchen table reading the series). It is rich with textures and scenes that revealed to me your loving commitment to your work.

I agree your commitment to detail and the artistry of the series was insane, but it is the kind of insane that propels us all forward. It inspires and yields greater results beyond your initial effort. We, the kids and I, love the series and thank you for your effort. I commend you for your love of your work and am inspired.

See you around,
Mike McCrory

> Jeez, all that insane work feels **WORTH** it, when I get a nice letter like this!

CONGRATULATIONS, ALEC, ON A MOMENTOUS ACHIEVEMENT! NOT CUTTING YOUR BEARD (THOUGH THAT MUST BE LIBERATING), BUT FINISHING BASEWOOD! HOW PERFECT THAT IT NEARLY OVERLAPS WITH THE DAWN OF A NEW YEAR!

THANK YOU SO MUCH FOR THE COMPLIMENTARY COPIES OF PHASE 7 AND YOUR ALL-AROUND GENEROSITY AS A CREATOR — FOR CONTRIBUTING TO THE MEDIUM AS AN INSTRUCTOR AND GIVING SO MUCH ENERGY TO YOUR STUDENTS, FOR SHARING SUPPORT AND OPTIMISM WITH OTHER CARTOONISTS, FOR BEING A ROLE MODEL, A MENTOR, AND A BIT OF A CRAZY MAN. I'M HUMBLED BY YOUR EXAMPLE!

AS A FELLOW WARRIOR DOING LONG-FORM COMICS, I SALUTE YOUR VICTORY. AND LIKE YOU, I AGREE THAT THE PLEASURE AND CELEBRATION OF COMPLETION IS DIVING INTO WHAT'S NEXT. I'M THIRSTY TO SEE WHAT YOU HAVE UP YOUR SLEEVE. AND TO SEE BASEWOOD COLLECTED IN ONE GORGEOUS VOLUME.

SO HERE'S TO YOU AND YOUR COMICS AND TO 2012!
WITH ADMIRATION,
CRAIG THOMPSON

St. ALEC defeats the dRAGON!
Craig 2 Jan 2012

THANKS

IF, SOMEHOW, YOU HAVE NOT SEEN CRAIG'S LATEST MASTERPIECE, **HABIBI**, YOU NEED TO GO FIND A COPY! IT IS, WITHOUT A DOUBT, THE MOST BEAUTIFULLY DRAWN GRAPHIC NOVEL OF ALL TIME. CRAIG IS ALREADY HARD AT WORK ON HIS NEXT **THREE** PROJECTS, AND I KNOW THAT I AM NOT ALONE IN SAYING THAT I CAN'T WAIT TO SEE WHAT HE COMES UP WITH NEXT. THE ADMIRATION, SIR, IS MUTUAL!

THE PHASE 7 SUBSCRIBERS!

MY MOTHER, FATHER AND SISTERS

ALL MEMBERS OF WEEZER, PAST AND PRESENT, FOR BEING THE GREATEST BAND EVER!

KARL KOCH FOR ALL HE DOES, AND MYKEL AND CARLI ALLEN (RIP)

KEVIN HUIZENGA FOR HALFTONE HELP

JASON SHIGA, AARON RENIER, JON CHAD AND GREG MEANS FOR THEIR FRIENDSHIP AND SUPPORT

MY WIFE, CLAIRE, FOR MORE THINGS THAN I COULD LIST HERE.

www.alec-longstreth.com

#018 - $3.00

ALEC LONGSTRETH

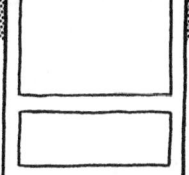

ISSUE EIGHTEEN
P.O. BOX 11207 OAKLAND, CA 94611
alec@alec-longstreth.com

I USUALLY USE THIS SPACE TO TALK A LITTLE BIT ABOUT WHAT IS CURRENTLY GOING ON IN MY LIFE, AND, UH... WELL, 2013 HAS BEEN A DOOZY SO FAR!

LAST YEAR, ON THE DAY BEFORE THANKSGIVING, MY GIRLFRIEND CLAIRE WAS DIAGNOSED WITH THYROID CANCER. THAT NIGHT I ASKED HER TO MARRY ME AND WE WERE WED ON JANUARY 14TH 2013. MY MAIN PRIORITY THIS YEAR HAS BEEN TO TAKE CARE OF CLAIRE. NOT ONLY BY BEING THERE FOR HER COUNTLESS TESTS AND THROUGH HER SURGERY AND RADIOACTIVE IODINE TREATMENT, BUT ALSO BY PUTTING SOME OF MY PERSONAL PROJECTS ON HOLD SO THAT I COULD FOCUS ON PAYING WORK TO HELP CHIP AWAY AT THE MEDICAL BILLS. I'M HAPPY TO SAY THAT CLAIRE IS DOING GREAT, AND THE DOCTORS SAY THAT ALL HER TREATMENTS DID WHAT THEY WERE SUPPOSED TO, SO CLAIRE IS IN THE CLEAR!

NOW THAT THINGS ARE GETTING BACK TO NORMAL AROUND HERE, IT'S TIME TO TACKLE SOME OF THOSE NEGLECTED PROJECTS. AT THE TOP OF THAT LIST IS MY FIRST GRAPHIC NOVEL **BASEWOOD!** I AM CURRENTLY SETTING UP A KICKSTARTER CAMPAIGN TO FINALLY GET ALL FIVE CHAPTERS OF BASEWOOD COLLECTED INTO ONE HANDSOME VOLUME. IF THIS SOUNDS LIKE SOMETHING YOU WOULD BE INTERESTED IN SUPPORTING, PLEASE HEAD OVER TO MY WEBSITE FOR ALL THE DETAILS. I WOULD REALLY APPRECIATE YOUR SUPPORT!

I HAVE ALSO BEEN DUTIFULLY PLUGGING AWAY AT "WEEZER FAN," PART TWO OF WHICH YOU ARE CURRENTLY HOLDING. I HOPE THAT YOU ENJOY IT!

—ALEC OAKLAND, CA

PHASE 7 #018 – AUGUST 2013. ENTIRE CONTENTS (INCLUDING ALL ART AND STORIES) COPYRIGHT ©2013 BY ALEC LONGSTRETH, UNLESS OTHERWISE NOTED (FOR INSTANCE, **BELOW**). NO PART OF THIS PUBLICATION (EXCEPT SINGLE PANELS FOR REVIEW PURPOSES) MAY BE REPRODUCED WITHOUT THE WRITTEN PERMISSION OF ALEC LONGSTRETH. DEAR GEFFEN, PLEASE DO NOT SUE ME!
FIRST PRINTING – 600 COPIES

BONUS! WEEZER CREDITS! ALL PINKERTON SONGS, THE B-SIDES "MYKEL AND CARLI" AND "SUSANNE," AND "HOLIDAY" FROM THE BLUE ALBUM WERE WRITTEN BY RIVERS CUOMO, PUBLISHED BY E.O. SMITH MUSIC (BMI). "SURF WAX AMERICA" FROM THE BLUE ALBUM WRITTEN BY RIVERS CUOMO AND PATRICK WILSON, PUBLISHED BY E.O. SMITH MUSIC (BMI) AND FIE! PUBLISHING (BMI).

weezer fan
PART TWO by ALEC LONGSTRETH

WEEZER'S SECOND ALBUM, "PINKERTON" WAS RELEASED ON SEPTEMBER 24TH, 1996.

AT THE TIME I WAS A JUNIOR IN HIGH SCHOOL, OUT IN THE SUBURBS OF SEATTLE, WASHINGTON....

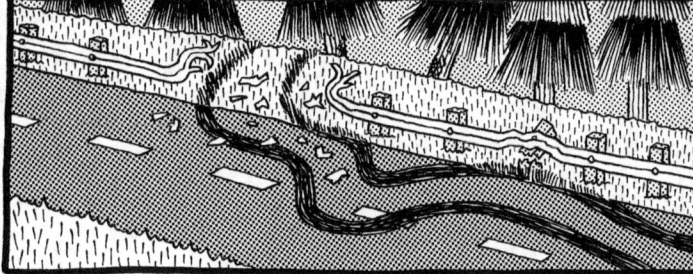

The bus parked out back then Karl and Pat's wife, Jen came to chat with us.

"We made this..."

"Thank you. I'll take it up to them."

Karl had to go inside to get set up for the sound check.

"I'll try to get them to come say hi afterwards."

A while later we heard them warming up through the wall.

"They're playing "Susanne!""

↑ my favorite Weezer song

Eventually the building went quiet again.

KNOCK KNOCK KNOCK

I FOUGHT MY WAY BACK TO THE MIDDLE OF THE CROWD, WHERE I COULD LISTEN TO THE MUSIC WITHOUT FEAR OF BODILY HARM.

WEEZER FOLLOWED "ACROSS THE SEA" WITH "HOLIDAY" FROM THE BLUE ALBUM.
"I CAN'T BELIEVE I'M ACTUALLY WATCHING THEM PLAY THIS SONG!"
HOLIDAY FAR AW LET'S

THEY POWERED THROUGH "GETCHOO," "NO ONE ELSE," "THE GOOD LIFE," "WHY BOTHER?," "NO OTHER ONE," "BUDDY HOLLY" AND "PINK TRIANGLE." I SANG ALONG TO EVERY SONG AT THE TOP OF MY LUNGS.
I'M DUMB, SHE'S A LESBIAN! I THOUGHT I HAD FOUND THE ONE

THEN, AFTER A ROUSING RENDITION OF THE "DUKES OF HAZARD" THEME SONG, BRIAN JUMPED ON THE MIC.
"THIS IS ONE OF OUR B-SIDES. IT'S CALLED 'SUSANNE.'"
OH... MY... GOD....
THUMP

THERE IS NOTHING QUITE LIKE SEEING YOUR **FAVORITE** BAND PLAY YOUR **FAVORITE** SONG. THE SOUND OF IT FILLED ME WITH ELATION.
SUSANNE YOU'RE ALL THAT I WA F A GIRL

THEY FINISHED OFF THE SET WITH "SAY IT AIN'T SO," "UNDONE" AND ANOTHER B-SIDE, "YOU GAVE YOUR LOVE TO ME SOFTLY."
WEEZER! WOO! YEAH!

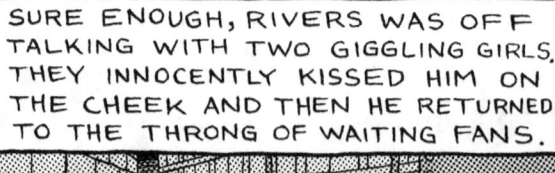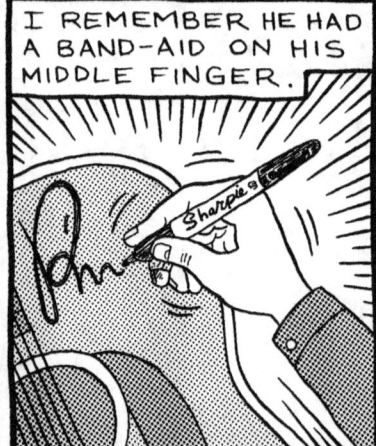

NOTES

I LEFT FOR COLLEGE A YEAR AFTER THAT WEEZER CONCERT, AND IN DOING SO, LOST TRACK OF MY WEEZER FRIENDS ALLISON REIBEL AND ERIC HOLL. IN MARCH 2012 I TRACKED THEM BOTH DOWN USING THE INTERNET. WE HADN'T SPOKEN SINCE THAT FATEFUL SUMMER NIGHT IN 1997.

I INTERVIEWED THEM INDIVIDUALLY, USING SKYPE. I COULD NOT HAVE DONE THIS ISSUE WITHOUT THEM! NOT ONLY DID THEY REMEMBER ALL KINDS OF LITTLE DETAILS FROM THAT DAY, THEY ALSO UNEARTHED AN AMAZING TREASURE TROVE OF REFERENCE MATERIALS. ON THESE PAGES YOU CAN SEE SOME OF THE PHOTOGRAPHS FROM THAT DAY, WHICH ALLISON AND ERIC HAD SAVED. THESE WERE GREAT, NOT ONLY FOR THEIR SENTIMENTAL VALUE BUT ALSO BECAUSE THEY HELPED ME DRAW **EXACTLY** WHAT PEOPLE WERE WEARING THAT DAY.

EVEN BETTER, ERIC SENT ME A BOOTLEG RECORDING HE HAD OF THE **ACTUAL** CONCERT THAT WE HEARD THAT NIGHT. THE SOUND QUALITY IS PRETTY BLASTED OUT AND IT'S MISSING "YOU GAVE YOUR LOVE TO ME SOFTLY" BECAUSE ERIC HAD TO FLIP OVER THE TAPE, BUT IT ALLOWED ME TO CONFIRM THE SET LIST AND PROVIDE **DIRECT QUOTES** FROM THE BAND, WHEN THEY TALKED INBETWEEN SONGS.

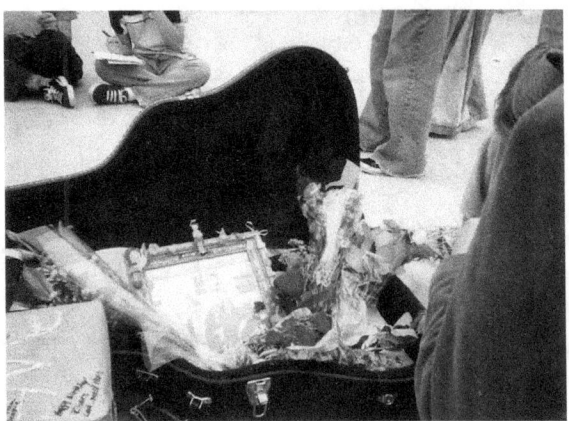

WHILE DOING ALL OF THE RESEARCH FOR THIS ISSUE, I ALSO DISCOVERED A MISTAKE I HAD MADE PREVIOUSLY.

A WEEK OR SO AFTER THE CONCERT ALLISON MAILED ME A COPY OF HER PHOTO OF ME AND RIVERS, WHICH IS ON THE BACK COVER. IT HAS ALWAYS BEEN ONE OF MY PRIZED POSSESSIONS.

IN 2006 I UPLOADED THE PHOTO TO FLICKR. I LABELED IT AS BEING TAKEN IN **1996** BECAUSE I KNEW IT WAS FROM THE PINKERTON TOUR, AND PINKERTON CAME OUT IN SEPTEMBER 1996.

IN 2010, I WAS CONTACTED BY WEEZER'S ASSISTANT, SARAH C. KIM, TO SEE IF I WOULD BE WILLING TO INCLUDE THE PHOTO IN **THE PINKERTON DIARIES**. I SAID IT WAS FINE WITH ME, AS LONG AS THEY COULD GET ALLISON'S PERMISSION. IN AN ATTEMPT TO BE HELPFUL, I ALSO LOOKED UP THE PINKERTON TOUR ON **WEEZERPEDIA**. I SCROLLED DOWN THE PAGE UNTIL I SAW "NOVEMBER 6TH, 1996 - SEATTLE, WA DV8." THIS WAS THE INFORMATION I **MISTAKENLY** PASSED ON TO SARAH. UNFORTUNATELY, THE PHOTOGRAPH WAS PRINTED IN THE BOOK ON PAGE 184, UNDER THE 11/6/96 ENTRY. IN THE TOP PHOTO (AT THE SHORECREST HIGH SCHOOL CONCERT - **ARGH!**) RIVERS CLEARLY HAS SHORT HAIR, WHEREAS IN ALLISON'S PHOTOS RIVERS HAS LONG HAIR. IT'S KIND OF CROPPED IN THAT PHOTO, SO IT'S EASY TO SEE WHY MY MISTAKE WAS NOT CAUGHT. I AM SO SORRY FOR THIS BLUNDER!

IT WAS NOT UNTIL I INTERVIEWED ALLISON AND ERIC THAT I REMEMBERED THERE HAD BEEN **TWO** SEATTLE

WEEZER CONCERTS, NINE MONTHS APART. I THINK NOVEMBER 6TH, 1996 WAS SO TRAUMATIC FOR ME, I TRIED TO BLOCK IT FROM MY MEMORY! ALLISON'S PHOTO **SHOULD** HAVE APPEARED ON PAGE 228 OF **THE PINKERTON DIARIES**. IN THE TOP PHOTO ON PAGE 229 RIVERS HAS LONG HAIR AND HE IS EVEN WEARING THE SAME SHIRT! AGAIN, THIS IS **MY** FAULT. I'M SORRY!

NOT ONLY WAS IT GREAT TO RECONNECT AND REMINISCE WITH ALLISON AND ERIC, AS YOU'RE ABOUT TO SEE, I GOT SOME GREAT LETTERS AND EMAILS FROM OTHER WEEZER FANS IN RESPONSE TO **WEEZER FAN: PART ONE**. PLEASE, KEEP 'EM COMING! IT'S A LOT OF FUN FOR ME TO HEAR ABOUT OTHER PEOPLE'S EXPERIENCES WITH MY FAVORITE BAND!

THE THIRD (AND FINAL!) PART OF **WEEZER FAN** WILL TELL THE STORIES OF EVERY WEEZER CONCERT I'VE SEEN SINCE 1996, IN OHIO, NEW YORK AND VERMONT. I'M HOPING TO HAVE THAT DONE IN EARLY 2014. ONCE THOSE SELL OUT I WILL THEN COLLECT ALL THREE ISSUES INTO ONE VOLUME. THAT'S MY PLAN AND I'M STICKING TO IT!

WEEZERLY YOURS,

ALE LONGSTRETH
WF #2660

THESE PHOTOS ARE ©1997 ERIC HOLL, ALLISON REIBEL AND/OR WHOEVER TOOK THESE PHOTOS!

LETTERS
P.O. BOX 11207 OAKLAND, CA 94611

NOTE: LETTERS TO PHASE 7 BECOME PROPERTY OF THE COMIC AND ARE ASSUMED INTENDED FOR PUBLICATION IN WHOLE OR IN PART (UNLESS OTHERWISE INDICATED).

JUST READ THE NEW WEEZER PHASE 7... DUDE, IT WAS **AWESOME!** THANKS SO MUCH FOR HOOKING ME UP, AND THANKS IN ADVANCE FOR THE ADDITIONAL COPIES! THEY WILL DEFINITELY GO TO GOOD USE — I WILL GET COPIES TO THE BAND AND MATT, AND THE BAND'S MANAGER DANIEL FOR SURE. AND I WANT TO GIVE MY GIRLFRIEND JENNIFER ONE AS SHE HAS BEEN A WEEZER FAN SINCE THE LATE '90s. I'LL THINK ABOUT WHO TO GET ANY OTHER ADDITIONAL COPIES TO. TODD SULLIVAN COMES TO MIND. RIC OCASEK TOO.

I WILL PROMOTE THIS ISSUE (AND PARTS TWO AND THREE AS THEY COME OUT) ON THE WEBSITE AND OUR "SOCIAL MEDIA OUTLETS" (BARF) TOO. I FEEL YOUR STORY IS BOTH "TYPICAL/UNIVERSAL" OF WEEZER FANDOM AS I'VE WITNESSED IT, BUT ALSO VERY UNIQUE AS YOU HAVE BOTH A GREAT MEMORY, GREAT ATTENTION TO DETAIL, CAN TELL A STORY REALLY WELL, AND HAVE AN EXCELLENT SENSE OF SELF — I SEE YOUR PERSONALITY SHINE THROUGH AT ALL THE AGES YOU DEPICT YOURSELF. IT NEVER FEELS LIKE A "FLASHBACK," IT FEELS LIKE YOU ARE ZIPPING BACK AND FORTH THROUGH TIME, RECOUNTING EVERYTHING AS IT IS HAPPENING IN THE PRESENT TENSE. MAYBE YOU TOOK REALLY DETAILED JOURNALS ALL THOSE YEARS. I SURE WISH I COULD READ MY OWN HANDWRITING SOMETIMES. ANYWAY, THANKS AGAIN ALEC!

—KARL KOCH

WOW, THANKS KARL! IT'S A REAL THRILL FOR ME TO KNOW THAT THE GUYS FROM WEEZER WILL SEE THESE ISSUES OF PHASE 7. THAT MEANS **A LOT** TO ME! AS EVERYONE SAW IN THIS ISSUE, KARL IS A BIG PART OF WHAT KEEPS THE WEEZER WORLD TURNING. HE PLAYS AN IMPORTANT ROLE IN PART THREE OF "WEEZER FAN" SO YOU'LL SEE HIM AGAIN!

DEAR ALEC,

A LITTLE WHILE AGO I HAD A DREAM THAT I WENT TO A BOOKSTORE WITH THE MOST AMAZING SELECTION OF COMICS, AND THE BEST PART WAS THAT THEY HAD AN ENTIRE SECTION DEVOTED TO WEEZER FAN COMICS. I SUPPOSE IT WAS FATE THEN, THAT WHEN I WAS VISITING CHICAGO I WENT TO QUIMBY'S AND FOUND YOUR ZINE.

I WANTED TO WRITE YOU AND TELL YOU THAT READING "WEEZER FAN" WAS QUITE A MOVING EXPERIENCE. ALTHOUGH I'M PARTIAL TO PINKERTON MYSELF, BOTH OF WEEZER'S FIRST TWO ALBUMS HAD A BIG IMPACT ON ME. I THINK YOU NAILED IT IN THE SECTION ABOUT "IN THE GARAGE." WEEZER IS A BAND THAT PEOPLE FIERCELY LOVE (RATHER THAN MERELY LIKE) BECAUSE RIVERS CAN CHANNEL THE FEELINGS OF ISOLATION AND LONELINESS THAT COMES WITH BEING AN OUTSIDER INTO ASS-KICKING ROCK AND ROLL. IT'S NOT ONLY RELATABLE, IT'S EMPOWERING.

I ALSO REALLY ENJOYED THE SEGMENT ABOUT SINGING "BUDDY HOLLY"

AT KARAOKE — "BUDDY HOLLY" HAS TOTALLY BECOME MY SIGNATURE KARAOKE SONG AS WELL. THERE WAS ONE MAGICAL JAPANESE KARAOKE BAR IN MY HOMETOWN THAT ACTUALLY HAD "ACROSS THE SEA," AND IT'S BECOME MY MISSION IN LIFE TO FIND THAT SONG AT KARAOKE AGAIN!

THE SEGMENT ABOUT "SAY IT AIN'T SO" RESONATED WITH ME AS WELL. BEING FROM SOUTHERN CALIFORNIA I HAVE SPENT MANY A LONG, SOLITARY CAR RIDE SINGING MY HEART OUT TO WEEZER.

THE PART OF YOUR ZINE THAT TOUCHED ME THE MOST, THOUGH, WAS "ONLY IN DREAMS." THOSE MOMENTS WHERE EVERYTHING IS STRIPPED AWAY AND IT'S ONLY ABOUT THE CONNECTION BETWEEN YOU AND THE MUSIC — THAT'S WHAT LOVING MUSIC IS ALL ABOUT.

ANYWAY, I SUPPOSE THIS WAS ALL A LONG WAY OF SAYING THAT I LOVED YOUR ZINE, SO MUCH THAT I WANTED TO WRITE YOU A LETTER AND TELL YOU HOW MUCH I APPRECIATED IT. I THINK IT'S PRETTY AMAZING THAT THE BLUE ALBUM IS ALMOST 20 YEARS OLD (!) AND IT'S STILL TOUCHING PEOPLE AND BRINGING PEOPLE TOGETHER. I'M LOOKING FORWARD TO THE NEXT PART OF "WEEZER FAN," AND I THINK YOU INSPIRED ME TO CREATE A WEEZER FAN COMIC MYSELF!

TAKE CARE,
HANNAH WATANABE-ROCCO
BROOKLYN, NY

> THANKS FOR THIS HEARTFELT, HANDWRITTEN LETTER, HANNAH. I HOPE THAT YOU **DO** MAKE A WEEZER FAN COMIC, I WOULD LOVE TO READ IT!

DEAR MR. LONGSTRETH,
I JUST RECEIVED, READ, LOVED AND RE-READ YOUR PHASE 7 ISSUE ABOUT WEEZER. OOO-EE-OOO DID I LOVE IT! IT'S HARD TO REALLY EXPLAIN HOW CLOSE TO MY HEART YOUR STORIES WERE TO ME. LIKE YOU, I AM A HARD CORE WEEZER FAN.

I LEARNED ABOUT THEM IN 2000, WHEN I WAS IN JUNIOR HIGH SCHOOL. UP TO THAT POINT, I ACTUALLY DIDN'T CARE MUCH FOR MUSIC. THANKS TO YOU, I HAVE A STORY I'M GOING TO COERCE ONE OF MY ARTIST FRIENDS INTO DRAWING. MY OWN "WEEZIN' FOR BEING." (HAR HAR).

BY THE WAY, I'M IMMENSELY JEALOUS OF YOUR WEEZER FAN CLUB CARD. ARGH. SERIOUSLY, IT BURNS.

I HEARD THAT THIS IS PART ONE OF A TRILOGY? CONSECUTIVELY? OR SPREAD OUT AS PHASE 7 GOES ON? NOW I'M VERY CURIOUS OF YOUR PINKERTON EXPERIENCE, AND SO ON.

ANYWAYS, MUCH LOVE TO YOU AND YOURS, AND I HOPE TO SEE MORE OF YOUR WORK!

SINCERELY,
NATHAN SCHULZ
ANAHEIM, CA

P.S. I GOT TO MEET RIVERS CUOMO AND I **DIDN'T** VOMIT ON HIM IN EXCITEMENT! BETTER THAN I THOUGHT I'D DO!

> HA HA, GLAD TO HEAR THAT YOU KEPT IT COOL, NATHAN. YOU'LL SEE ME TRY TO DO THE SAME THING IN PART THREE!

HEY ALEC,
SO — I WAS IN A SILVERLAKE COMIC STORE AND FOUND PHASE 7 #017. I WAS VERY EXCITED. IT'S GREAT OBVIOUSLY AND AS SOMEONE WHO SPENT YEARS OBSESSED WITH OBSCURE POP-PUNK BANDS THAT NO ONE REALLY KNEW, I

could relate to your excitement about finding fellow fans.

I decided to write you because when I found your comic something dawned on me—even though we weren't really good friends, you really had an influence on stuff I did. I remember getting paired with you my freshman year during commencement and you showed me where you drew comics and told me about 24-hour comic day. Years later in Minneapolis I surrounded myself with indie comic kids and asked about the craft until someone showed me the basics. I don't draw a lot, but when I do I am very happy and don't mind taking a year or more to finish an issue. I wanted to send you both comics I've made since if it wasn't for meeting you I'm not sure I would be doing this.

I also remember seeing you play a show at the Cat and the Cream, just you and a guitar. When I saw that I thought—hey, I could do that! I played a show at the Cat my senior year with a dozen or so songs I wrote at Oberlin. After that I formed a band in Minneapolis called Bla Bla Black Sheep. I'm sending you that CD too.

I'd been in bands since I was a high schooler. I've written songs for a long time but I really admired how passionate your songs were. I forgot about seeing that show of yours until I saw that Phase 7 comic and I thought about how your show made me think acoustic was cooler than electric.

Anyway, I'm not saying all this to creep you out or suggest you were some idol I modeled my hobbies after. Far from it, it's just that I think I really admired how you just did cool things and it always looked easy and fun. That's how things should be, right?

A few times I've stumbled across other comics you did and I've seen you pop up in other people's comics too—usually when they talk about that comic school in Vermont. It's kind of weird to hear about someone you knew in that way, but pretty rad too. These days I'm in Los Angeles working for a public radio station. Whatever you are doing in Oakland, I hope you're still having fun. I'm looking forward to your next comic... Pinkerton is my favorite Weezer album. Then Blue, then either Maladroit or Raditude.

    Keep up the good work and take care,
    Sanden Totten
    Los Angeles, CA

Great to hear from you, Sanden! I'm honored that I played some small part in encouraging your creative pursuits. I agree that making stuff should be **FUN**. Drop Sanden a line to order issues 1 & 2 of his zine "It Will All Make Sense Tomorrow" and the Bla Bla Blacksheep album: sandentotten@hotmail.com

THANKS

The Phase 7 subscribers / my mom, dad and sisters / Sunny Wu and Isaac Baker for additional memory assistance / Weezer, Karl Koch and Mykel & Carli (RIP) / Jason Shiga, Greg Means, Jon Chad, Aaron Renier and James Sturm / above all, my wife Claire Sanders ♡

www.alec-longstreth.com

#019 - $4.00

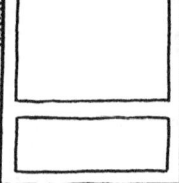

ALEC LONGSTRETH

ISSUE NINETEEN
P.O. BOX 534 ALAMEDA, CA 94501
alec@alec-longstreth.com

CLAIRE AND I HAVE MOVED YET AGAIN — THIS TIME ONLY ABOUT FOUR MILES FROM OUR OLD PLACE. I DO HAVE A NEW P.O. BOX, SO PLEASE TAKE NOTE ABOVE BEFORE SENDING ME ANY MAIL!

YOU ARE HOLDING IN YOUR HANDS THE THIRD AND FINAL INSTALLMENT OF MY "WEEZER FAN" TRILOGY. MY GOAL, WHEN I STARTED THIS STORY, WAS TO HAVE MORE FUN MAKING COMICS. WELL, MISSION ACCOMPLISHED! IT'S BEEN A BLAST DRAWING COMICS ABOUT MY FAVORITE BAND, AND CONNECTING WITH OTHER WEEZER FANS ALONG THE WAY.

IT'S A GREAT TIME TO BE A WEEZER FAN! THEIR NINTH STUDIO ALBUM, "EVERYTHING WILL BE ALRIGHT IN THE END" WILL BE RELEASED OCTOBER 7TH, 2014! (I'VE BEEN RACING AGAINST THE CLOCK, TRYING TO GET THIS ISSUE DONE BEFORE "EWBAITE" DROPS!). FROM WHAT I'VE HEARD SO FAR, THE ALBUM SOUNDS LIKE IT'S GOING TO BE **EPIC**.... BUT YOU KNEW I'D SAY THAT!

PHASE 7 #020 IS ALREADY OUT (WHOOPS! SORRY ABOUT THAT!) SO THE NEXT ISSUE TO BE RELEASED WILL BE PHASE 7 #021. THAT ONE'S ALL ABOUT MY EXPERIENCES GROWING MY BEARD AND HAIR OUT FOR THREE AND A HALF YEARS. I'VE GOT THE NEXT DOZEN ISSUES AFTER THAT ALL FIGURED OUT, I JUST NEED TO FIND THE TIME TO MAKE THEM. I'M FEELING GOOD ABOUT PHASE 7 THESE DAYS — LIKE THE BEST IS YET TO COME! I HOPE YOU'LL ALL CONTINUE TO CHECK OUT WHAT I'VE GOT COMING DOWN THE PIPELINE. I APPRECIATE YOUR READERSHIP!

— Alec   ALAMEDA, CA

PHASE 7 #019 — OCTOBER 2014. ENTIRE CONTENTS (INCLUDING ALL ART AND STORIES) COPYRIGHT © 2014 BY ALEC LONGSTRETH, UNLESS OTHERWISE NOTED (FOR INSTANCE, **BELOW**). NO PART OF THIS PUBLICATION (EXCEPT SINGLE PANELS FOR REVIEW PURPOSES) MAY BE REPRODUCED WITHOUT THE WRITTEN PERMISSION OF ALEC LONGSTRETH. BLA BLA BLA.
FIRST PRINTING — 500 COPIES

BONUS! MUSIC CREDITS: ALL SONGS WRITTEN BY RIVERS CUOMO, PUBLISHED BY E.O. SMITH MUSIC (BMI) EXCEPT AS NOTED: "MISS SWEENEY" WRITTEN BY RIVERS CUOMO AND SARAH C. KIM, PUBLISHED BY E.O. SMITH MUSIC (BMI). "SURF WAX AMERICA" BY RIVERS CUOMO AND PATRICK WILSON, PUBLISHED BY E.O. SMITH MUSIC (BMI) AND FIE! PUBLISHING (BMI). "LET IT ALL HANG OUT" WRITTEN BY RIVERS CUOMO, JERMAINE DUPRI AND JACKNIFE LEE, PUBLISHED BY E.O. SMITH MUSIC (BMI), SHANIAH CYMONE MUSIC/EMI APRIL MUSIC (ASCAP) AND CHRYSALIS MUSIC. "THE END" IS BY THE BEATLES (DUH). "BLEED AMERICAN" IS BY JIMMY EAT WORLD.

weezer fan

PART THREE by ALEC Longstreth

WEEZER'S 1996 ALBUM "PINKERTON" DID NOT SHARE THE COMMERCIAL SUCCESS OF THEIR FIRST, SELF-TITLED RELEASE. THUS BEGAN THE WEEZER "DARK AGES," A SPAN OF TIME WITH VERY FEW UPDATES FROM THE BAND. SOME FANS EVEN THOUGHT THAT WEEZER HAD BROKEN UP.

IN REALITY, THEY WERE DOWN, BUT NOT OUT! AND LUCKILY, THEY STILL HAD PLENTY OF GOOD MUSIC LEFT IN THEM....

#
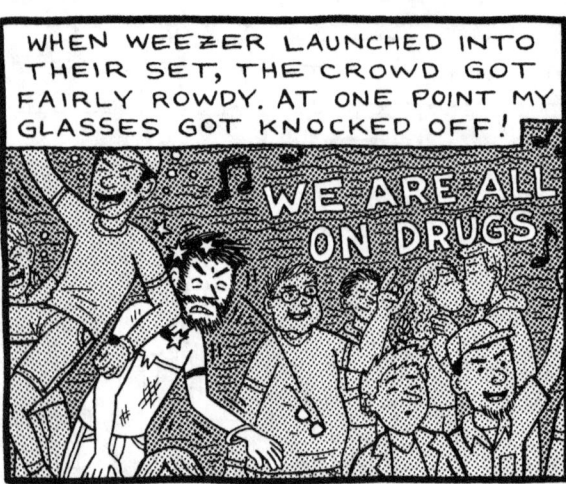 

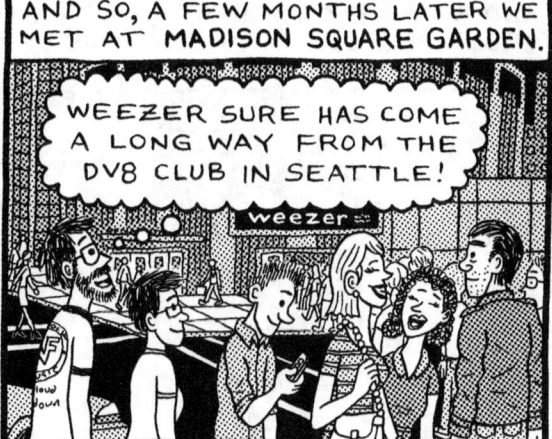

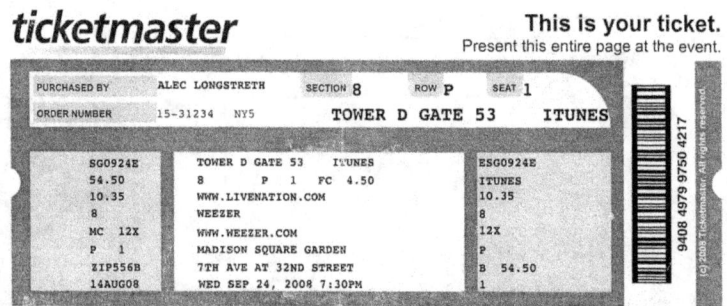

I CAME UP WITH DOZENS OF GIFT ICONS, WHICH I SENT TO KARL IN BATCHES. I JOKED THAT I HAD BEEN TRAINING FOR THIS ILLUSTRATION ASSIGNMENT FOR MY ENTIRE LIFE!

THE GIFT ICONS NEVER REALLY TOOK OFF ON THE SITE, BUT THESE ILLUSTRATIONS DID NOT GO TO WASTE!

I TOOK ONE ICON FOR EACH SONG FROM THE BLUE ALBUM AND PINKERTON AND RECOLORED THEM USING A LIMITED PALETTE INSPIRED BY THE ALBUM COVERS. I ALSO MATCHED THE ORIGINAL ALBUM LETTERING.

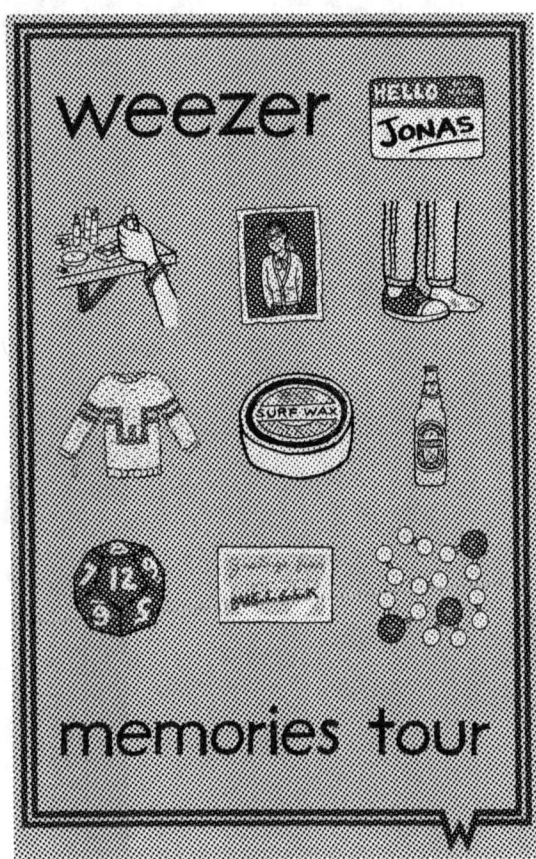

NOTES

3:1 – OLD RIVER ROAD!

14:4 – THESE GLASSES DID NOT HAVE LENSES, SO THIS WASN'T A **HUGE** DEAL, BUT I STILL WOULD HAVE BEEN BUMMED IF THEY GOT CRUSHED.

15:1 – WWW.HEROESONLINE.COM/HEROESCON/

17:1 – WWW.FALYNNK.COM

24:4 – THIS SHOW IN VERMONT WAS MIKEY'S PENULTIMATE PERFORMANCE WITH WEEZER. HE PLAYED "UNDONE" WITH THEM ON JULY 29TH, 2011 (ALONG WITH THE FLAMING LIPS). TRAGICALLY, MIKEY DIED ON OCTOBER 8TH, 2011 AT THE AGE OF FORTY.

31:2 – WWW.WEEZER.COM (DUH)

34:3 – **NO!** I DO NOT HAVE ANY COPIES OF THE MEMORIES TOUR POSTERS FOR SALE. SORRY, I ONLY DREW THEM!

36:5 – I MET JASON CROPPER TWICE: ONCE IN 1997 AT A **CHOPPER ONE** SHOW IN BELLVUE, WA AND AGAIN IN 2013, BACKSTAGE AT A WEEZER SHOW IN SAN FRANCISCO.

LETTERS

ALEC,
  I AM LISTENING TO THE BLUE RIGHT NOW. GETTIN' IN DEEP. THERE REALLY IS SOMETHING ABOUT IT THAT FEELS LIKE A DANGEROUS CAR. COULDN'T PUT DOWN THE WEEZER PHASES BECAUSE THEY BROUGHT BACK THAT RUSH. I HOPE IT PLEASES YOU THAT, LIKE A DESPERATE PLEA IN AN L.A. TRAFFIC JAM, YOUR WORK HAS ME TUNING IN TO YOUR STATION. ON MY SECOND SPIN TODAY. PROLLY LOOKIN' AT A THIRD SOON. THANKS SO MUCH FOR SINGING SO LOUD. OH, AND SORRY I NEVER RE-FORWARDED THE LETTER I SENT TO VERMONT REGARDING THE BLACK HOLE. THOSE ELEGANTLY BOTCHED, ACHING AND UNFINISHED SONGS HIT ME JUST THE RIGHT WAY DURING A LOW EBB. I THINK YOU MUST BE A VERY VALIANT PERSON TO BE ABLE TO REACH TO PEOPLE THE WAY YOU DO. I THINK IT'S RARE. HOOK ME UP WITH YOUR UPCOMING ISSUES? NOT SURE HOW TO SUBSCRIBE, SO I JUST WROTE A RANDOM AMOUNT.

  – NICHOLAS GUREWITCH
  ROCHESTER, NY
(A CHECK FOR $19.94 WAS ENCLOSED)

THANKS FOR ALL THE KIND WORDS, NICK! THIS LETTER MEANT A LOT TO ME FOR TWO REASONS:
1) NICK IS ONE OF THE FUNNIEST CARTOONISTS ALIVE. IF, SOMEHOW YOU HAVE NOT READ HIS WEBCOMIC **THE PERRY BIBLE FELLOWSHIP**, NOW IS THE TIME:
  WWW.PBFCOMICS.COM
2) ON A LONG TRAIN RIDE TOGETHER IN 2008, NICK ASKED ME ABOUT THE FIRST TIME I EVER HEARD WEEZER. I HAD NEVER TOLD ANYONE THAT STORY BEFORE,

AND TELLING IT TO NICK, AND EXPERIENCING HIS ENJOYMENT OF THE STORY, WAS THE BEGINNING OF ME WANTING TO DRAW THIS COMIC!

HEY BUD,

LOVED THE WEEZER STUFF! I TOO WAS A MEMBER OF THE WEEZER FAN CLUB, CIRCA 1994 OR '95 BUT I NEVER SAW IT AS THE EXTREME SOCIAL RESPONSIBILITY THAT YOU DID. I JUST PUT THAT CARD IN A DRAWER AND ENJOYED THE NEWSLETTER. I WAS IMMERSED IN ZINES HEAVILY AT THAT TIME SO IT PROVIDED A NICE BACKDROP TO MAKE WEEZER APPEAR PLEASANTLY LESS CORPORATE THAN I HAD PREVIOUSLY THOUGHT OF THEM. NOW I WONDER WHAT NUMBER I WAS.

ALMOST TWENTY YEARS LATER AND I'VE STILL NEVER SEEN WEEZER PLAY. THEY WERE JUST HERE, PLAYING FOR FREE BUT NO ONE WOULD GO WITH ME. BUT A CRAZIER OPPORTUNITY: IN 1999 MATT AND PAT WOULD COME TO SHOWS AT THE PUNK HOUSE WHERE I LIVED, THE DUSTBIN, AND COMPLEMENT THE BANDS! I WAS TOTALLY STAR STRUCK. BUT WHEN I LOOKED IN THE LP, THE FAN CLUB ADDRESS WAS LITERALLY A PRIVATE MAILBOX COMPANY ON THE SAME STREET I LIVED ON.

I'VE ALWAYS BEEN A BIGGER FAN OF READING ABOUT MUSIC THAN LISTENING TO IT AND THAT'S ONLY INTENSIFIED IN RECENT YEARS, SO YOUR COMICS WERE A BREATH OF FRESH AIR ON SOMETHING I LONG FORGOT I LOVED, PINKERTON. AND THEY MADE ME DUST OFF THE LP!

SO THANK YOU FOR THAT. AND MY GIRLFRIEND ELLY, WHO GENERALLY HATES COMICS BUT LOVES YOURS, WOULD NEVER FORGIVE ME IF I DID NOT MENTION THAT SHE IDENTIFIED THAT EVERY BIT OF TRAGEDY IN BOTH ISSUES IS RELATED TO THE HORRORS OF CARS AND THAT **THAT** IS THE HIDDEN NARRATIVE OF YOUR WEEZER HISTORY. PLEASE DISSECT THAT IN PART FOUR.

DID YOU READ **NOTHING FEELS GOOD** BY ANDY GREENWALD? BEST ANALYSIS OF WEEZER AND CUOMO I'VE SEEN, OTHER THAN INTERPERSONAL BAND DYNAMICS, WHICH IT DOESN'T GET INTO BUT ARE EXHAUSTIVELY EXPLORED ELSEWHERE.

THANKS FOR ADDING SOME GREAT, HONEST STORYTELLING TO THE CANON AND I AM SO EXCITED TO READ PART THREE.

APOLOGIES THAT THIS COMES FROM FAST-FLYING THUMBS ON MY IPHONE RATHER THAN A PROPER LETTER BUT IT'S LATE AND I'M EXHAUSTED AND THIS MUCH TEXT GIVES ME HAND CRAMPS WHEN I WRITE WITH A PEN.

BETTER WRAP THIS UP BEFORE I SOUND MORE LIKE A FOGEY THAN I AM.

VERY BEST,
JOE BIEL
PORTLAND, OR

THANKS FOR THE LONG EMAIL, JOE! IT WAS GREAT TO READ ABOUT SOME OF YOUR EXPERIENCES WITH WEEZER. I'M GLAD TO HEAR THAT MY COMICS ENCOURAGED YOU TO BREAK OUT PINKERTON! JOE IS THE MASTERMIND BEHIND MICROCOSM PUBLISHING AND HAS ALSO MADE TONS OF ZINES AND DOCUMENTARIES AND ALL SORTS OF OTHER COOL STUFF. HEAD OVER TO: WWW.MICROCOSMPUBLISHING.COM TO CHECK IT ALL OUT!

DEAR ALEC,
  YESTERDAY AT A COMIC BOOK STORE, I DISCOVERED PHASE 7. IT WAS #018, AND THE MAIN REASON IT STUCK OUT TO ME WAS SEEING A FAMILIAR PICTURE: NONE OTHER THAN THE COVER OF PINKERTON!!! RIGHT THEN, I STARTED THINKING OF A TIME — ALMOST TWO YEARS AGO — WHERE A FEW OF MY FRIENDS WERE IN LOVE WITH THE ALBUM. IT WAS MOSTLY BETWEEN A GIRL WHO I BELIEVE GOT INTO IT RECENTLY, AND A BOY REMEMBERING IT, AND WE ALL KNEW HOW CUTE THEY WOULD HAVE BEEN TOGETHER. THEY GOT MY OLDER SISTER AND HER BUDDY INTO IT — WHICH MADE ME THINK IT MUST HAVE BEEN GOOD. EXCEPT FOR A FEW SONGS I COULD REMEMBER (ACROSS THE SEA, PINK TRIANGLE, AND I VAGUELY RECALLED EL SCORCHO), I HAD NEVER LISTENED TO IT — UNTIL TODAY, WITH YOUR COMIC CONVINCING ME. AND IT WAS EVEN BETTER THAN I HAD EXPECTED — **ESPECIALLY** THE GUITAR WORK. BUT, WHILE READING THE LYRICS, I REALIZED I HAD HEARD EL SCORCHO IN THAT SAME COMIC STORE JUST YESTERDAY. AND I REMEMBERED HOW THAT SAME BOY AND GIRL CONSIDERED THAT "THEIR SONG," AND LISTENING TO IT MADE ME UNDERSTAND THEM A LITTLE BETTER. AND I ALSO FELT WHAT I THINK COULD HAVE BEEN SOME OF THE HAPPINESS WE WERE ALL EXPERIENCING AT THE TIME. AND THAT SENSE OF UNITY IS MY FAVORITE ELEMENT OF MUSIC. SO THANK YOU FOR BRINGING THIS BACK TO ME, AS I'M GOING TO PUT "FALLING FOR YOU" ON A MIX-TAPE FOR MY BEST FRIEND. I DON'T THINK IT WAS THE BEST, BUT SOME OF THE WORDS, WERE APPROPRIATE.

—THANK YOU,
LEAH OGDEN
CROFTON, MD
P.S. SORRY FOR MY HANDWRITING!

> I FORGIVE ALL SLOPPY HANDWRITING WHEN I GET A NICE LETTER LIKE THIS IN THE MAIL! **WHOOPS!** I FORGOT TO PUT MY "LETTERS NOTICE" ABOVE, SO I'M GOING TO SNEAK IT IN RIGHT HERE: **NOTE:** LETTERS TO PHASE 7 BECOME THE PROPERTY OF THE COMIC AND ARE ASSUMED INTENDED FOR PUBLICATION IN WHOLE OR IN PART (UNLESS OTHERWISE NOTED). **OKAY—** BACK TO THE LETTERS!

HI ALEC,
  THANKS SO MUCH FOR GETTING PHASE 7 #017 & #018 IN THE MAIL SO FAST, THEY ARRIVED SAFELY EARLIER TODAY. REALLY ENJOYED THEM BOTH TREMENDOUSLY, AS A BIG-TIME WEEZER AND COMIC FAN.
  THIS PARTICULAR STORY IS A UNIQUELY FUN EXPERIENCE, IN THAT WHILE READING, ESPECIALLY THE WAY #017 IS STRUCTURED, I BASICALLY HAVE THE ALBUM PLAYING IN MY HEAD AS A MENTAL SOUNDTRACK, ANY TIME A SONG'S TITLE AND/OR LYRICS ARE MENTIONED.
  I WAS GRADUATING HIGH SCHOOL WHEN THE BLUE ALBUM CAME OUT, AND IT WAS A SIMILARLY SPECIAL ALBUM FOR ME. IT REMAINS ONE OF THE ALL-TIME BEST FULL ALBUM EXPERIENCES. I RARELY PUT IT ON WITHOUT LISTENING THROUGH THE WHOLE THING. AND PINKERTON IS ANOTHER, STILL A BIT UNDERAPPRECIATED, CLASSIC IN ITS OWN RIGHT.
  THANKS AGAIN AND CONGRATS ON A COUPLE MORE GREAT ISSUES OF PHASE 7. LOOKING

FORWARD TO PART THE THIRD!
CHEERS,
CHRISTIAN MEESEY
LOS ANGELES, CA

P.S. THANKS FOR GETTING THESE CLASSIC ALBUMS STUCK GOING THROUGH MY HEAD AGAIN. TIME TO ADD THEM BACK TO MY CAR CD PLAYER'S ROTATION FOR SOME LOUD L.A. COMMUTING SINGALONGS.

> I'M GLAD TO HEAR HOW MUCH YOU ENJOYED THE COMICS, CHRISTIAN! I WAS IMPRESSED BY CHRISTIAN'S SKETCH BLOG. CHECK IT OUT AT: WWW.MEESIMO.BLOGSPOT.COM

THANKS

WELL, FIRST OFF, I'D LIKE TO THANK ALL THE GREAT WEEZER FANS WHO WROTE ME A LETTER, SENT ME AN EMAIL OR SAID HELLO TO ME AT A COMICS SHOW. THE BEST PART ABOUT WORKING ON THIS PROJECT HAS BEEN HEARING **OTHER** PEOPLE'S WEEZER STORIES. WEEZER HAS PUT OUT **SO** MANY ALBUMS AND GONE ON **SO** MANY TOURS, IT'S REALLY AMAZING TO ME, TO REALIZE HOW MANY LIVES THEY HAVE TOUCHED WITH THEIR MUSIC.

SECONDLY, I'D LIKE TO THANK **ALL** THE MEMBERS OF WEEZER FOR BEING SUCH A GREAT BAND AND FOR BRINGING SO MUCH JOY INTO MY LIFE. I'D ESPECIALLY LIKE TO THANK RIVERS, PAT, BRIAN AND SCOTT, THE PRESENT MEMBERS OF WEEZER, WHO ARE CURRENTLY ON THE ROAD, PROMOTING "EVERYTHING WILL BE ALRIGHT IN THE END." I'VE GOT MY TICKETS, AND CAN'T WAIT TO ROCK OUT TO WEEZER ONCE AGAIN! =W=♡

AS EVER, I HAVE TO THANK KARL KOCH FOR ALL HIS HARD WORK DOCUMENTING THE SHOWS AND KEEPING THE FANS UP TO DATE WITH THE LATEST INFO. I TRULY BELIEVE THAT **KARL** IS ONE OF THE MAIN REASONS IT IS SO MUCH FUN BEING A WEEZER FAN.

I'D ALSO LIKE TO THANK ALL THE FOLKS WHO RUN <u>WEEZERPEDIA.COM</u> IT WAS AN INVALUABLE RESOURCE FOR THIS PROJECT, AND THE EXTENSIVE TOUR DATES, SET LISTS AND KARL'S CORNER ARCHIVES HELPED MAKE MY STORIES MUCH MORE ACCURATE.

ONE LAST TIME, I'D LIKE TO THANK MYKEL & CARLI ALLEN (RIP). THEY WELCOMED ME IN TO THE WEEZER COMMUNITY TWENTY YEARS AGO, AND I WISH THEY WERE STILL HERE TODAY, SO I COULD SEND THEM THESE ISSUES. I HOPE THEY WOULD HAVE LIKED THEM.

AFTER THAT, IT'S THE USUAL SUSPECTS:

THE PHASE SEVEN SUBSCRIBERS FOR STICKING WITH ME

MY MOTHER, FATHER AND SISTERS

GABE CARLETON-BARNES FOR HIS CAN-DO ATTITUDE!

JASON SHIGA, FOR DRAWING WITH ME

JON CHAD, FOR KEEPING UP THE SIDE-PROJECT MOMENTUM (MISS YOU, DUDE!)

GREG MEANS, MY FELLOW ROAD WARRIOR

AND LASTLY, MY WONDERFUL WIFE CLAIRE, WHO TOLERATES MY WEEZER-MANIA

	2010-09-02 Essex Junction, VT - Champlain Valley Expo
1	Epic Intro
2	Hash Pipe
3	Troublemaker
4	Undone
5	Surf Wax America
6	Memories
7	Perfect Situation
8	Dope Nose
9	Say It Ain't So
10	Brian's Theme
11	Island in the Sun
12	El Scorcho
13	My Name is Jonas
14	Beverly Hills
15	Hot for Teacher
16	Pork and Beans
17	MGMT/Lady Gaga
18	I Want You To
19	Buddy Holly

www.alec-longstreth.com

www.alec-longstreth.com

 ONLINE ORDERING!

 WEB ONLY 24-HOUR COMICS!

 SNEAK PREVIEWS OF UPCOMING ISSUES!

THANKS FOR READING SOME OF MY COMICS. I HOPE YOU ENJOYED THEM! —Alec

THIS BOOK IS SELF-PUBLISHED
WITH **PRIDE!** IT WAS PRINTED
ON DEMAND, USING

MORE COPIES CAN BE PURCHASED AT
http://lulu.com/spotlight/longstreth
OR
http://alec-longstreth.com/comics

www.ingramcontent.com/pod-product-compliance
Lightning Source LLC
LaVergne TN
LVHW081354060426
835510LV00013B/1813